HIDDEN TREASURES

SOUTH YORKSHIRE VOL I

Edited by Donna Samworth

First published in Great Britain in 2003 by
YOUNG WRITERS
Remus House,
Coltsfoot Drive,
Peterborough, PE2 9JX
Telephone (01733) 890066

HB ISBN 0 75434 151 8
SB ISBN 0 75434 152 6

FOREWORD

This year, the Young Writers' Hidden Treasures competition proudly presents a showcase of the best poetic talent from over 72,000 up-and-coming writers nationwide.

Young Writers was established in 1991 and we are still successful, even in today's technologically-led world, in promoting and encouraging the reading and writing of poetry.

The thought, effort, imagination and hard work put into each poem impressed us all, and once again, the task of selecting poems was a difficult one, but nevertheless, an enjoyable experience.

We hope you are as pleased as we are with the final selection and that you and your family continue to be entertained with *Hidden Treasures South Yorkshire Vol I* for many years to come.

The Poems

SEASONS OF WEATHER

Dancing daffodils of spring and all
Growing so big and getting so tall
Lambs bleat at the sight of their birth
In the lush green abundance of the fields of Perth.

Summertime is on, people are on the beaches
Other people though are picking pretty peaches
The sun is blazing down upon the sea
Everyone is happy, including you and me!

Blustery winds of autumn that blow,
Through the meadows that really can flow!
It's harvest time for farmers and me and you,
The colours, red, yellow, brown and orange too!

Winter's snow is the very chill
Makes animals quiet and still
Slippery ice is the very warning
Frost on the garden as the day is dawning.

All the seasons different to each other,
They have their own tricks one after another.
Sunny, snowy, windy all have different features
Seasons of weather, observed by many creatures!

James Evans (10)
Bessacarr Primary School

BEING A CAT

Sat on the wall all day,
Watching the sun rise and fall,
Being a cat is awful,
It's no fun at all!

People going, 'Here puss,'
All day and all night
But at least I'm not a dog,
At least I did something right.

Because I hate those stupid mongrels,
That come charging down the street,
Before they go inside their house,
They have the mud wiped off their feet.

Nasty, smelly dogs,
No one touches my feet.
Being a cat is OK, I suppose,
Because I get the best quality meat.

Sophie Clayton (11)
Bessacarr Primary School

WATER

If it had a smell it would be
Clear, clean, crisp and fresh.
If it had a shape it would be
Big, wide and spacious.
If it had a best friend it would be
The warm, golden sun.
If it had a hobby it would be
Swimming and fishing.
If it had a job it would be
A doctor.
If it ever left us
People would die!

Tiffany Belnavis (10)
Bessacarr Primary School

WINTER

Snow is falling,
Caterpillars crawling,
Ponds are frozen over,
People picking clover,
Snow is falling!
Snow is falling!

Car windows frozen hard,
People are dropping Christmas cards,
The time has come to open presents,
People eating the Christmas pheasant,
Snow is falling!
Snow is falling!

Nicole Steed (10)
Bessacarr Primary School

TV

I watch TV all day,
While is stayed there to lay.
I saw a show,
Which was slow,
And so I laid there all day.

The very next day,
I was still there to lay,
I was still watching TV,
Until I needed a wee,
And then I said 'Bye-bye.'

Matthew Ho (10)
Bessacarr Primary School

AUTUMN

Red, yellow, green and brown are the colours of the leaves
All falling in sheaves!
The mornings are getting misty,
And the nights are getting colder.

The geese are starting to fly,
High in the sky.
They don't like the snow,
But I do!

Fruit is getting sweeter,
All tasty but weather-beaten.
Mellow pears and rosy plumbs,
De-icing the car makes my fingers go numb!

I scrunch up my toes in bed,
Trying to find some warmth,
Autumn, good morning,
Summer, goodnight!

Eve Newton (10)
Bessacarr Primary School

PICTURE FRIGHT

I was drawing a mini picture,
A picture of my mum,
But my teacher said:
'Why that looks like a little crumb!'

So I drew an orange and green blob,
It was the picture of my mum!
But she had to tell me how to draw a
Proper mum. (Oh bum!)

But my teacher was terrified,
Because at half-past three,
An orange and green blob
Collected me!

Edwina Chan (10)
Bessacarr Primary School

I DON'T KNOW WHAT TO WRITE

I don't know what to write,
A poem it's got to be,
I will be here all night,
I'll miss my tea.

I don't know what to write,
I don't know what to say,
I've got to sit and type,
I'll be here all day.

Thomas Earnshaw (9)
Bessacarr Primary School

MY CAT

Purring catnap,
On the fence
Pounce!
And catch
Eat it up,
Back to bed
Purring catnap
On the fence.

Inside, feeding time
Licking lips and purring,
Fish and milk
What a delight.

In the room,
Playing with strings
Balls are bouncing, cats are pouncing.

Back to bed
Sleepy head.

Philippa Burton (9)
Bessacarr Primary School

HORSES

Horses and foals eating grass on the hill,
Big shire horses working for the mill.

Horses and ponies all like hay,
And all the foals like to play.

The farrier comes to give your horse a shoe,
Horses have saddles, bridles and stirrups too.

Some horses would like to pull a cart,
And some have such a loving heart.

Some people like cats and some like rats but I like horses most,
At least they do not boast!

Having my own would be so great!
It would be my best mate!

Kyrie Birkett (10)
Bessacarr Primary School

FRISBEE

Frisbee flying in the air
Whizzing round like an aeroplane
Whizzing here, flying there,
'Watch out for the window pane.'
Little boy running around
Whizzing here, flying there
Sees the frisbee on the ground
Throws it high in the air
He has no time to stop and stare.

Sarah Horsley (9)
Darton Primary School

A HAUNTED HOUSE

Step in through the ghostly gates
Be quiet or beware.

We're going to peep and stare
Inside the haunted house.

Wizards, witches and trolls
Glow in the darkness of the haunted house.

Aargh they're after us!
Get out!

Thomas Garforth (10)
Darton Primary School

CAT IN THE HOUSE

There's a cat in the house,
It might get the mouse.
Make sure Mum doesn't see,
I hope it doesn't bite me.
I don't like that cat,
It's heading for the mat
Run little mouse run!

Alice Mullaney (9)
Darton Primary School

BUBBLES

Bubbles, bubbles, everywhere,
Pop them if you dare,
Going here, going there,
Going everywhere.
They pop on walls, they pop on houses,
They pop on anything they see.
Do you see that bubble floating in the sky?
Oh dear
It has
Popped
On me!

Isabelle Bentley (9)
Darton Primary School

A PUPPY CALLED POP

There was a puppy called Pop,
She liked to jump, skip and hop,
She was a happy little puppy was Pop.

Her coat was black, tan and fluffy,
She was a tiny bundle of fun,
She liked to lie in the sun,
Then after a while she'd hop up again,
And play until she'd flop in her bed,
At the end of the day.

She is a friendly pup is Pop,
I love her with all my heart.
She is a strong little might,
But still cries a bit at night.

She wanders here and wonders there
Yet she never strays,
She is a loyal little pup is Pop.

Shauni Cawthorne (9)
Darton Primary School

THE BIG, FAT CAT

I saw a cat going in a flat,
Someone get the big, fat cat.
Huge and smelly on the street,
Going in a flat as you see.
Going up the stairs
People falling down the stairs
People trying to get it
Even me
As you see.
All the people from the street
That cat, that huge, fat cat
Very smelly, squishy just like jelly
Everyone going for the cat
Someone get the big, fat cat.

Lewis Copley (9)
Darton Primary School

WEED

There was a girl who sowed a seed
But all that grew was a weed.
The weed was tall amongst the grass,
It was small but it had a red flower
That grew by the hour.
People came from all around
To see the flower that grew from the ground
There came a boy who decided to pick
Within an hour he was sick,
His body turned red
And then he was dead.

James Lodge (10)
Darton Primary School

A DIM GOBLIN LIFE

I'm a little goblin green and white
Sometimes I gather my friends and we fight.
We ride the squig herd
Which may sound absurd
But life's not so dim
And nor is it grim.
To ride with my friends
All green and white
Riding the squigs
In our goblin fight.

Thomas Wilkinson (9)
Darton Primary School

ALIENS AND STARS

Aliens, aliens live on the moon.
Aliens, aliens live on Mars.
Aliens, aliens live on Mercury.
Aliens, aliens hide in stars.

Stars, stars make history,
Stars, stars make pictures like
Lions, unicorns, centaurs and crabs.

Thomas Wilford (9)
Darton Primary School

ON THE FARM

I wear green wellies
To go to the farm
I have to be careful
So's not to come to any harm.
Uncle Phil drives the tractor
And ploughs the field.
Uncle Stewart sows the seed
So the crops we grow we can yield.

Grant Gemmell (9)
Darton Primary School

THE SCARY GHOST

Once on a dark, dark night
I saw a castle that gave me a fright.
I decided to open the big, round door
And was shocked to see snakes on the floor.
I thought it was best to move away,
And leave the snakes for another day.
Then I went down the spooky hall,
And saw a scary ghost on the wall.
I ran and ran and ran
Until I saw him again near the fan.
I knew I'd had enough so I ran to my mum,
Then woke up in bed, I knew I'd been so dumb.

Scott Mason (9)
Darton Primary School

MY HERO STONE COLD

Stone Cold's his name
Wrestling's his game.
He's fighting Chris Jericho
They hit and bash
They make a crash.
Bang, he's landed on the floor.

Along comes Triple H to help Stone Cold
And gets him in the sleeper hold
They grab and grapple
Pull and push
In comes the grapple gear
Then there is a very big cheer.
The fight is over, the belt is won
Stone Cold's the winner, he's my number one.

Thomas Horsley (9)
Darton Primary School

THE WOODEN AEROPLANE

A wooden aeroplane
Needs wind, wind, wind
To fly into the
Midnight
Sky.

Fly, fly, fly
The plane
Flies high
Into the
Cloudy
Sky.

Into the sky the
Aeroplane flies, high into
The dark midnight
Sky.

Oliver Hayes (9)
Darton Primary School

PAPER PLANES

Paper planes glide and turn,
They go fast and speedy,
They do tricks like turns and flips.
Paper planes go up, down, round
And all the way round.

Matthew Heald (9)
Darton Primary School

THE OLD DOG

There is an old dog,
He lives on my street,
He's very scruffy,
His name is Pete.

He lives next door
In the garden shed,
It's nice and warm
In his snugly bed.

But if you ever bought him
And you kept him for long
I can reassure you
You'd get no sleep
Because of his terrible loud song.

Rebecca Anne Peace (9)
Darton Primary School

DEEP BLUE SEA

Under the sea,
There can be
Two fishes,
Some sharks,
Some seals,
A sunken boat,
And the reflection of the stars in the night.
So dive right in,
There just might be,
Something under the sea,
You will never see again.

Amy Jo Wood (10)
Darton Primary School

FOG

As morning dawned it was there
Silence struck the autumn air,
Fog sank to the ground.

Stillness whispered to death-shocked trees
Bewitching the air that we breathe.

Hope arrives as sun works with wind
Sun melts misty fog,
Wind shoots holes like bullets into
The fog's grey heart.

Sun beams down all day long singing
Its joyful song,
Wind blows a gentle breeze not one
That will make you freeze.

Fog returns, spreads its poison once again,
Rules over and blows its icy breath
Across the field.

Fog arrives for revenge
Engulfs slowly but silently
And is back to rule again.

Ryan Sykes (11)
Doncaster Road Primary School

FOG

As morning dawned
He was there
Covering the landscape with
His giant hands.

Creeping across valleys
Like he's hunting.

Gulping up fields
Like a pig who hasn't eaten in days.

Quietly slithering through
Gardens, fields, valleys and streets.

Sun shines its brightest
Shine ever.

Fog burning, so then he flees.
His quickest.

Sun sets . . . moon rises . . . fog comes.

So silence struck the night-time air.

Ashley Dawson (10)
Doncaster Road Primary School

FOG

As morning dawned it was there,
Covering the countryside with its thick blanket
Putting a spell on the trees.
Spreading its mixture of whites, silvers and greys,
Forbidding anything to be seen.
A flash of gold light and the sun is awake,
The sun commands the fog to leave,
The fog softly creeps away.
Night rolls back again and the sun is asleep,
The fog stares at the countryside
With its gleaming silver eyes,
It takes over the countryside once again.
Everything is silent
As the fog swirls around covering everything in its path.
It makes everything look deserted.

Rachel Everett (11)
Doncaster Road Primary School

FOG

As morning dawned it was there,
As the fog crept into the valleys and the hillside.
Lurking about over the valleys.
Everything in its path will get
Covered.
Drifting through the valley,
Covering the trees and the
Valleys.
So quiet and still covering
The hill.
The blanket of fog
Is white, grey and silver.
It is deserted. Nobody
Was there. It looked like
It didn't care.
After a while,
The sun came and gave
A smile.
Then the fog disintegrates
And it fails.
Then night falls
And the fog creeps
Over the wall.

Jessica Brown (10)
Doncaster Road Primary School

FOG

Silence struck the morning air . . .
With fog covering everywhere, white fog spreading
Over the hillside.
Standing still like ghostly shadows
As the fog smoothly wraps itself around everything
Sunlight shining on the fog as it disappears
The fog is behind the hillside hiding behind the corner
With a nasty grin waiting to get its own back
As darkness falls over the hillside.

Sophie McKenzie (11)
Doncaster Road Primary School

FOG

Silence struck the morning air
Thick fog everywhere
Spread over like butter on bread.
Silence took over the countryside.

As the wind rolled in, it chased
Away the silver fog,
On which had settled on treetops.
Ground covered like an
Enormous piece of white paper.

Then the raging wind raced off to bed.
The thick engulfing fog waits until its moment and
Reincarnates
To get its revenge!
To conquer the countryside
Once again.

Lyndsay Barton (10)
Doncaster Road Primary School

FOG

Silence struck the morning air,
It conquered the hillside,
Like a dull blanket swallowing the valleys
And the tree trunks.
Finally the sun comes and chases it
To a far distance.
It smoothly creeps all over.
Silently it disintegrates.
Night is falling, back it comes to get its revenge!

Lauren Goulding (11)
Doncaster Road Primary School

FOG

As morning dawned it was there . . .
Lurking around the countryside air,
Of course it was the fog!
Drifting at its own pace,
The fog crept around the valley,
So silent until a flash of the sun came,
Drift, drift until coming of night,
And don't reappear tomorrow.

Laura Copley (10)
Doncaster Road Primary School

FOG

Silence struck the morning air . . .
As he swiftly crept his scaly hand
Around the white valley.
And skid on the icy lake,
People were silent with a deathly hush.
But sunset rose once again and chased the
Gloomy fog away!
But he stayed until it was silent so
He could get his revenge once again.

Lindsay Clayton (11)
Doncaster Road Primary School

FOG

Silence struck the morning air . . .
It was early morning
As horses were sleeping in the dark.
There was so many people just sleeping in their beds.
The fog was slowly slithering in the air
And just ten minutes later there was just silence
Like it had never been before.
It had been bad but never like this.
So that gave the fog time to get busy
Well it was left in peace.
Well it was left in peace.
The sun came and the sun went into the sea.
So the sun had time to set.
The fog went as fast as he could into the air
It was night so the fog came and the sun got revenge.
The sun came back.
The sun said, 'Get out of my sight.'
And the fog said, 'I've failed again.'

Laura Ackroyd (10)
Doncaster Road Primary School

FOG

Silence struck the morning air
Icy ground covered everywhere,
Outside it was deserted and silent.
Fog had engulfed everywhere
Nothing to see, nothing to hear.
Fog crawling like a white polar bear.
Later, the wind came and chased the fog away,
That night when everyone was
Asleep, the fog slithered
Back for revenge.

Ben Land (10)
Doncaster Road Primary School

FOG

Silence struck the morning air
The fog stretches himself away,
Blocking the countryside everywhere,
The fog thinks he can do whatever he wants,
But then it's time for the sun to come out
And fight it away.
You've been busy while I was away.

Besfort Terholli (10)
Doncaster Road Primary School

FOG

Silence struck the morning air
Slowly and softly trees froze to the ground
As the fog swiftly stretched its hand
Among the countryside with trees sleeping
Through foggy winter's nights
With blackness of the dead rising from the cemetery
In the black winter's nights.

Dawn approaches to the morning air
And chases the fog away with a boot of light.

Fog chases the sun back and takes
Its place for its destiny and revenge.

Hayley Hibbert (11)
Doncaster Road Primary School

FOG

As morning dawned it was there
A silent draft of fog did steer
For it was ready to spread out its wings.
Two hours later the sun came out
You should have seen her beam and sprout,
Her rays heated the foggy fields,
And took that mist clear away,
But as night dawned the fog peered round the corner.
And when she saw the moon which smiled,
She conquered back to the dark shivering fields
To stretch out her frosty legs once again
And fog up the roads with her icy toes.
So as the night is deserted and still,
And the cold drifts in from the night
The fog once again gets ready to pounce.

Georgina Miller (10)
Doncaster Road Primary School

FOG

As morning dawned it was there,
Stretched its huge legs over the land
Showing no mercy.

The morning had no force to fight back,
As it threw its big, misty, silver blanket over the land.

The wind just sat lazily,
No sight of it.

The fog stood its ground
Slept silently in the morning air.

The first sight of the sun,
Takes the fog and burns it to
Crisp like a blowtorch.

Wind gets its strength back and sweeps the fog up.

But not far,
It waits round the corner till dark.

The sun is tired and sets in the sky,
Fog springs back into its place,
Back over the hillside.

As morning dawns it was there . . .

Matthew Brazier (11)
Doncaster Road Primary School

UNTITLED

There once was a young man called Lee,
Who got stuck up a tree.
The fire brigade
Came to his aid
But by then he got stung by a bee.

Michael Trickett (10)
Greenfield Primary School

THERE WAS A YOUNG BOY CALLED ADAM

There was a young boy called Adam
Who had a friend called Callum
They sat on a wall,
They had a great fall,
And were rushed to the hospital at Hallam.

Katie Wood (9)
Greenfield Primary School

THERE'S A MONSTER UP THE STAIRS

There's a monster up the stairs
I don't know what to do.
There's a monster up the stairs
And I know it's someone new.

There's a monster up the stairs
He's nearly at the top.
There's a monster up the stairs
I hear its footsteps stop.

There's a monster up the stairs
He might be very keen.
There's a monster up the stairs
And he also can be mean.

Brooke Wyatt (10)
Greenfield Primary School

Spring Haiku

Rabbits, cows and lambs.
Blossoms blooming on the trees.
Flowers start to grow.

Lauren Winder (10)
Greenfield Primary School

UNTITLED

There was an old man called Fred,
Who always slept in his bed
Until one day,
The bed gave way
And fell on the floor and Fred was dead.

Adam Graham (10)
Greenfield Primary School

SNOW HAIKU

White, silver and gold,
Snow is falling to the ground,
It is really cold.

Amelia Wingrove (10)
Greenfield Primary School

MY BEST FRIEND

My best friend is really cool,
She can beat me at everything including pool.
She eats chocolate spread
And bounces on her bed
That's before school.

She's got the best tackle ever
She's a nutter when we're together
She wears specs
Her sister's called Becks
And it's always Rachael and Heather.

She's got beautiful blonde hair,
She wins all her dares,
She's bouncy and fun,
She gets all her work done
I'm green with envy, greener than a pear.

Heather Steer (10)
Greenfield Primary School

UNTITLED

Trees are full of buds
Lambs hop and skip in the fields
When flowers blossom.

Warren Hopkinson (9)
Greenfield Primary School

TOM AND THE BOMB

There once was a boy called Tom,
Who discovered a very old bomb,
The bomb was loaded
And it suddenly exploded
And that was the end of poor Tom.

Thomas Peasegood (9)
Greenfield Primary School

FOR SUMMER HAIKU

Wearing shorts and shirts,
Holidays by the seaside
Swimming in the sea.

Carl Hewitt (9)
Greenfield Primary School

A FRIEND

My friend is seven feet tall
She can't even kick a ball
She bounces on her bed
But ends up bumping her head
I don't know why she bothers at all.

Although she is clumsy she is still my friend
And we will stick together till the end
She cheers me up when I am sad
But sometimes makes me really mad.

Rebecca Mott (10)
Greenfield Primary School

I LOVE HORSES

I love horses, I think they're sweet
I think some look very neat.

I love horses, some are tall
Some are big, some are small.

I love horses, they are fun
I can't beat them when I run.

I love horses, they eat hay
I love it when they gallop, away.

Stephanie Greasley (9)
Greenfield Primary School

UNTITLED

There was a young man called Ben
Who was always messing with his pen
He shook it about
All the ink came out
And he couldn't use it again.

Jamie Haigh (10)
Greenfield Primary School

MY BEST FRIEND

I have a best friend called Fred
Who was always bumping his head
He walked into a wall,
Which was very tall,
And ended up in a bed in a shed.

Lauren Chappell (10)
Greenfield Primary School

RIDDLE ME, RIDDLE ME

Riddle me, riddle me rot, tot, tote
A little wee man in a red, red coat
A staff in his hand a stone in his throat,
If you tell me a riddle I'll give you a
Goat!

Riddle me, riddle me rot, tot, tote
A cat on a lead, a man in a coat
If you tell me a riddle I'll give you a
Goat!

Kathryn Hinkles (9)
Greenfield Primary School

A TRIP TO THE PARK

I went to the park one day,
When I heard someone say,
'What do you do with your time?'
And I replied 'I'm just sublime.'

I was walking to the park one day
Doing what I do
When someone came up to me
And thought I had the flu.

I went to the park today
But now I am at home
Next time it's the summer holidays
I think I'll go to Rome.

I was walking to the park one day
Doing what I do
When someone came up to me
And thought I had the flu.

I'm going to the park tomorrow
Well I really, really hope
'Cause I can easily cope.

I was walking to the park one day
Doing what I do,
When someone came up to me
And thought I had the flu.

Nathania Daykin (10)
Hatfield Woodhouse Primary School

BREATHING

You breathe in the air,
Which is around everywhere,
Breathe life from the air.

Your air is stored, where?
In your lungs of course, that's where,
Lungs are in your chest.

Nathan Macpherson (10)
Kiveton Park Meadows Junior School

I WISH I WAS HOME

I hope I go home
Where it's nice and warm
In my nice, comfy chair
So please let me go
Here we go to the place I don't know.

In the camp it's horrible and cold
Where can we go
As we say we don't know
Singing for hope.

Here we go to the place I don't know
Oh please, oh please we pray for hope
Moaning all day, hoping are we
Everyone's there, no voices are heard.

Holly Walker (9)
Kiveton Park Meadows Junior School

THE TRUE HOLOCAUST

No butterflies fly there,
No birds sing aloud.
Only the rats dare to go there
Hangs over a dark cloud.
They're the camps of the holocaust
Where the Nazis take the Jews.
If you end up in a camp
It's never good news.
So please God put this to an end
'Cause all that happens there
Is lying, dying, sighing and crying
With people in despair.

David Brookes (10)
Kiveton Park Meadows Junior School

CONKERS

Gleaming conkers on the glorious tree
Choked in that deathly green cage
The boy comes acrimoniously;
And sets the imprisoned conkers free.
He treasures them in his pocket
The boy runs with glory.
When he gets home,
He polishes the gleaming conkers gently.
He puts them in a box and treasures them.

Antony Green (10)
Kiveton Park Meadows Junior School

THE HORSE CHESTNUT POEM

The tree stands unprotected,
Waiting for an enemy to approach.
The needle-like spikes guard
The gleaming, glossy jewel imprisoned inside.
The leaves rustle; a sign of danger!
An enemy is near,
The lethal spikes are on sentinel,
Watching as the intruder gets
Nearer and nearer,
As the boy gets closer
To the tree it sends a shiver down the trunk,
It makes the leaves sway; jittery.
The boy ransacks the tree
And steals a gleaming treasure.
He hastens away
Carrying a gleaming glossy jewel.
The tree sighs and moans in the wind.

Amie Bonsall (11)
Kiveton Park Meadows Junior School

HAIKU - THE BOOM

Chemicals and germs
Reproduction by system
You are made of bones.

Food and drink to live
Without the sun we will die,
We need to be warm.

Sam Downs (9)
Kiveton Park Meadows Junior School

I WILL PUT IN MY BOX...

I will put in my box ...
A butterfly flying
Through the blue sky
A turquoise one.

I will put in my box ...
A smooth stone that is breathing,
A shouting noise from the sea,
A rabbit sharing a story or two.

I will put in my box ...
Five silver wishes,
The last smile of my cousin,
My sister's first tooth.

I will put in my box ...
Six seasons and a cold sun,
The man on the moon riding a horse,
The cowboy riding the crescent.

I shall go horse riding in my box
In and out of the falling trees that
Are green, the colour of grass.

Rebecca Rigby (9)
St Michael's RC School, Barnsley

I WILL PUT IN MY BOX . . .

Light from a seemingly soundless sun
A dark, dying Japanese dragon.

I will place in my box . . .
The swinging of a lively locket,
A picture from the top of the Statue of Liberty,
The playful soul of a monkey.

I will put in my box . . .
Two pink wishes spoken in Japanese,
The last bullet before peace
And the first giggle of relief.

I will put in my box . . .
An eighth day and a red star,
A rich person in an old car,
A poor person in a brand new car.

My box is fashioned from oak wood,
Red admiral butterflies.
Its hinges are created from solid silver.

I shall win a fight in my box
Against Bruce Lee and take a champion's ransom of gleaming gold.

Callum McNally (10)
St Michael's RC School, Barnsley

MAGIC BOX

I will put in my box . . .
The sun when it shines like a sunflower,
The tip of a tiger's tongue touching my tooth,
The rapid rain falling to the ground.

I will put in my box . . .
A rock that cries,
A blade of greenest grass,
A snapping bark of a dog.

I will put in my box . . .
Two grand wishes spoken in Spanish,
The last words of my nannan,
The first words of my sister.

I will put in my box . . .
The thirteenth month,
A blue moon,
A king in rags,
A beggar in golden robes.

My box is blue like the bluest sky
With jade diamonds on top
With sides made from candles.

I shall swim in my box,
With the Atlantic dolphins,
Then be washed ashore
Onto a desert island.

Jade Reeder (9)
St Michael's RC School, Barnsley

I WILL PUT IN MY BOX . . .

I will put in my box . . .
A baby whimpering on a windy, wintry night,
A fiery, red-hot diamond straight out of lava,
Babies live a very long life.

I will put in my box . . .
A sparkling diamond singing out loud.
I will take a large rock
From a sandy beach,
A robin that flies off a glittery card.

A fiery wish spoken in Italian,
The last words from my great grandmother,
The bark from a puppy.

A thirteenth month with a red moon,
The farmer sings
And the pop star works on the farm.

My lid is covered in glitter,
It sparkles in the sun
With dreams underneath
And memories all around
The lid is made with snake skin.

I shall go swimming with dolphins in my box
And never come back.
I will live with dolphins in the ocean
I love my box.

James Mockford (10)
St Michael's RC School, Barnsley

ACTION!

I will put in my box . . .
A moving moth menacing a man,
Nine ninjas wrestle through nets
And myths realise their fortune.

I will put in my box . . .
A stuffed animal with a concerned heart,
A slight glimmer of the world's equator,
A shudder of a swallow swooping through the woods.

I will put in my box . . .
Three gentle wishes spoken throughout Lychenstein,
A ruby cursed wind that wakes the dead,
A push and a squeeze, a mother in labour.

I will put in my box . . .
A new world,
A human body in a tangled wood
And nature's animals indoors.

My box is woven with metal chains,
In the middle, an inspirational gem
With a lucky dip inside.

I shall ski in my box
And sail the seven seas
And sink with pride to the bottom of the ocean
Where I'll rest in peace.

Luke Simpson O'Regan (9)
St Michael's RC School, Barnsley

THE MAGIC BOX

I will put in the box . . .
Rosy red ripe apples in a tropical forest,
A beach full of people, building sandcastles,
The sound of the sparkling sea, splashing upon the shore.

I will put in the box . . .
A smooth pebble that breaths,
A cup of purest water from a mountain spring
And a dolphin making a huge splash.

I will put in my box . . .
Two bright blue wishes whispered in Spanish,
The last laugh of my grandfather
And the first time my cousin played out with me.

I will put in my box . . .
A thirteenth month and a bronze moon,
A bear in a basket,
A cat in a cave.

My box is fashioned with silver and gold stars all over
With memories in the middle.
The hinges are made out of crocodile teeth.

I shall swim in my box
Trying to find out all its secrets
Then I will end up on a warm, soft beach where I will lie in the sun.

Stacey Vodden (10)
St Michael's RC School, Barnsley

THE MAGIC BOX

I will put in the box . . .
A furry, fascinating, fierce cat
That catches innocent birds.

I will put in the box . . .
A crystal that will sing to me
And an elegant snow woman dancing on the ice.

I will put in the box . . .
Two pink witches whispering in Egyptian
And the first tooth from a baby
And the last fish in the sea.

I will put in the box . . .
A seventh season of a pink sun,
The fish sat on the throne
And a king beneath the sea.

My box is fashioned from
Silver, gold and steel,
With hearts on the lid and flowers in the corner.

I shall dance in my box,
On the slippery ice
And I will be washed away by the pink sea.

Shelby Golby (10)
St Michael's RC School, Barnsley

BEACH

I will put in the box . . .
The shiny pebble sparkles below the sun,
The smell of the fisherman's breath,
The tip of my toes touching my tongue.

I will put in the box . . .
A snake that will whisper to me,
A spoon full of the purest water,
The jump of a fury dolphin.

I will put in my box . . .
Three golden wishes spoken in German,
The last voice from my Nanan Alice,
My first front two teeth from being a baby.

I will put in my box . . .
The thirteenth month and a full moon,
A moon, the afternoon sky
And the sun in the midnight sky.

My box is fashioned with
Shapes overlapping each other,
With hearts on the lid and pockets in the corners
And the hand joints of a mouse.

I shall sit with my pebble
All day long until it's time to go home from the whitest beach
Under a white moon.

Rebekah Bailey (10)
St Michael's RC School, Barnsley

Rally Drive

I will put in the box . . .
A beautiful, bare beach in dazzling sunlight
A drifty rainforest up on the moon.

I will put in the box . . .
A scarecrow stuffed with corn
Starting to rumble in his thrashing belly.

I will put in the box . . .
Three violet Spanish wishes
Spoke to me by my first cousin.

I will put in the box . . .
A king in a dungeon,
A slave in a palace.

My box has a gold seal
With stars at the corners
And jokes on the sides.

I shall rally drive in the rainforest
Between the trees
In a BMW with white and blue stripes.

Dan Smith (10)
St Michael's RC School, Barnsley

I WILL PUT IN MY BOX...

I will put in my box . . .
The sound of the sea clashing to rocks on a summer sunny morning,
Ladybirds sitting on a nettle and a smile of my best family.

I will put in my box . . .
A shell that laughs on the beach,
A cold river floating along,
A slow bubbling fish.

I will put in my box . . .
Four golden wishes,
The hand of my great grandad
And the first baby's talk.

I will put in my box . . .
The ninth season with the sizzling hot sun,
Queens live on the streets and tramps live in palaces,
What a dream.

My box is made of shinny gold with lots of bubbles and wishes
All wrapped up safe and sound the colours are beautiful
Like the colours of the rainbow.

I will stuff in my box . . .
The sea clashing and I ride dolphins
On a sunny evening passing by and a little breeze
Swaying around until night-time
Comes around.

Elizabeth Caswell (9)
St Michael's RC School, Barnsley

LIGHT UP THE WORLD

The sun is round
But makes no sound.
Light up the world.

The sun is a fire blazing
And quite amazing.
Light up the world.

The sun is high
Towards it all the birds try to fly.
Light up the world.

The sun is a circle
Thank God, it's a miracle.
Light up the world.

Leigh Heald (10)
St Michael's RC School, Barnsley

THE SEA

The sea can be a killer,
It's the star of a really bad thriller.
You never know what lies beneath.

The sea can get insane
When it's been sailed on, thick, black paste.
You never know what lies beneath.

The sea carries all our waste
It often looks like black, thick paste.
You never know what lies beneath.

You never know,
You never know,
You never know what lies beneath.

Reece Phillips (11)
St Michael's RC School, Barnsley

SUMMER

Summer is when we build sandcastles
Near the sun, where it dazzles.
Time to get tanned.

On a holiday in Greece,
In the pool with my brother Reece.
Time to get tanned.

With my family at a barbecue . . .
Sausages, my brother just had two.
Time to get tanned.

Rebecca Anderson (10)
St Michael's RC School, Barnsley

KILLER

Swooping through the air with piercing eye
He watches patiently where rabbits lie.
He's a cunning killer.

A soon-to-be-departed rabbit is unaware
The killer is behind it with a mean, old stare.
He's a cunning killer.

A strike finishes the job and a meal is in hand,
For our peregrine falcon who rules the land.
He's a cunning killer.

After a long night's rest a new day awakes
With radiant beams that the new sun makes.
He's a cunning killer.

With sprawled out wings the killer comes round
With another day ahead he soars without sound.
He's a cunning killer.

Today is different for a goose is in sight
A stinging dive vanishes its day lights.
He's a cunning killer.

The day finishes, he's had a plump goose to eat,
He tried hard and deserved the treat.
He's a cunning killer.

Josh Batty (10)
St Michael's RC School, Barnsley

SHARKS

Its fierce staring eyes gleam through the sea,
With a great big wag of its tail, he's chasing after me!
I'd like to touch its razor-sharp teeth.

Its stinging rows of vicious teeth,
Are needle-sharp and deep underneath.
I'd like to touch its razor-sharp teeth.

He senses any drip of blood,
I won't but he certainly would.
I'd like to touch its razor-sharp teeth.

Sharks are predators they eat a human now and then
But I want to know when.
I'd like to touch its razor-sharp teeth.

Daniel Howe (9)
St Michael's RC School, Barnsley

STORMS

The lightning is shocking
Mum's only just hung out her stockings.
I wouldn't like to get struck by it.

A storm's on its way
The clouds have gone grey.
I wouldn't like to get struck by it.

There's a shiver down my spine
I do not feel fine.
I wouldn't like to get struck by it.

I hear the thunder strolling in
And the rain poured down, as if it's on tin.
I wouldn't like to get struck by it.

Jason Appleby (10)
St Michael's RC School, Barnsley

STARS

I look up at the stars at night,
And wonder how they shine so bright.
I wish that I could be up there,
And look down at the Earth and stare.
At all the countries, people and oceans,
That fill me with all sorts of emotions.

Amy Staniforth (11)
Ward Green Primary School

THE LIFE CYCLE OF WATER

The stream down below
The sun up on high,
The water evaporates
To the clouds in the sky.

The drops of water start to get fat
So come down as rain, pitter, pit, pat
They come down to Earth and give you a bath
Rain washes everything down even your path!

Water runs down your drain,
Then makes some small puddles,
But in this cycle of life,
It meets a few muddles.

Water gets drunk by dogs
Then by people
Gets tipped down the drain
Then runs in a stream by a steeple.

Runs down the stream
And into a river
Runs down to the sea,
Now water's a winner.

Now it's the end,
It's time for goodbye
Quick now start this again
The water's evaporating into the sky!

Danielle Matthews (9)
Ward Green Primary School

MY DAD

My dad's name is Phil Cooper,
To me he is super duper.

My dad has dark hair and sometimes he has a beard to match
He also has a small bald patch.

My dad acts silly with me and sometimes we pretend to fight,
But my dad always gives me a kiss goodnight.

My dad goes to work every morning whether it's raining or sunny
Just so that he can give my mum and me lots of money.

My dad takes me to McDonald's nearly every Thursday
I have a Happy Meal and Dad has a Coke
Because he is thirsty.

I love my dad.

Emily Cooper (9)
Ward Green Primary School

FIREWORKS

Catherine Wheels go round and round
Rockets go shooting from the ground,
Fire is burning and fireworks are popping,
All around Jumping Jacks are hopping,
Bang, bang, bang the fireworks are going
Up in the sky the fire is glowing.

Hannah Hutchinson (8)
Ward Green Primary School

BENEATH THE OCEAN

Deep in the depths of the ocean
There are exciting things to explore.

Pirate's sunken treasure
Lay in the shipwrecks on the ocean floor.

Coins of gold,
Rubies and precious stones in store.

Deep in the depths of the ocean
It's like a magic potion.

You will find something special
Like golden treasure.

Things full of pleasure
Deep in the depths of the ocean.

Natalie Jagger (8)
Ward Green Primary School

CATZ

Cats are the best
They are better than the rest
With loads of furry fur,
And a very gentle purr.
They sleep in the night,
They play in the day,
They eat in-between
What more can I say?

They can run for miles,
In all sorts of styles,
They go bonkers chasing conkers,
They are rough and tough when they want to be
Aren't they just like you and me.

Cats are my favourite type
Even though they are little tykes
Black, white, ginger, grey
You are sure to see every day.

Cats will always be my friend
And our friendship will never end.

Cats are purrfect!

Amy Walker (9)
Ward Green Primary School

LAZY DAISY

I have a pet whose name is Daisy,
She is a little hamster who is so lazy
And she'll roll herself into a ball,
Then you would not know that she is there at all.

Amy Cropper (8)
Ward Green Primary School

THE PUPPIES

My auntie has ten pups
When they have had their milk they get burps and hiccups.
They fit in the palm of your hand
They find something comfy to land
They don't open their eyes yet
But they still know their own little way
No matter what they do
I will still love them every day.

Amy Bergan & Amelia Pilkington (10)
Ward Green Primary School

JUMPY CUSTARD

If all the world was ice cream
And all the seas were mustard
And all the skies were apple pies
There wouldn't be any custard.
Which would be a pity because. . .
Frogs love it
Even when it's lumpy
They eat it hot
They eat it cold,
They eat it when it's nine days old!
Custard makes them jumpy.

Jack Wordsworth (8)
Ward Green Primary School

THE EAGLE

The eagle powerfully sores through the sky
Its sharp ferocious talons dangle as it flies
Its brown earth-coloured feathers, rest upon its wing
But people call it a big sparrow without a chirping sing.
The eagle's golden face holds a pair of cunning eyes
They glimmer and shimmer in the sunlight as off to a crag it flies.
Being a bird of prey it catches its meals with grace
Then drags it away to a quiet, lonely place.
The eagle's remote nest lies in wait for eggs
As they begin to crack their beak starts to appear
Then finally their legs.

Charlotte Worth (10)
Ward Green Primary School

A DAY AND NIGHT POEM

Day
The day is bright
So the world is light,
The grass is green,
And I have seen
People flying a kite,
With all their might,
You hear the wind blow,
You see the sun go.

Night
The night is dark,
You hear the dog bark,
The owl hoots,
The car toots,
It passes by,
The bats fly,
The night is a fright,
But the day is very bright.

Lauren Atkinson (9)
Ward Green Primary School

SECRET GARDEN

Up and up and up the stone steps
The white snow crunching under my feet
In the old oak a robin sings its song
As I walk further into the garden I sight a pond
Look! A frog, watch as it jumps into the water.

Lauren Conway (8)
Ward Green Primary School

HORSES

Tail swaying,
Always playing.

Apple muncher,
Carrot cruncher.

Neck biters,
Little fighters.

Stable sleeper,
Shoe keeper.

Show jumping,
Door thumping.

Lovely colour,
Carriage puller.

Rolling in mud
Misunderstood.

Katherine Shepherd (11)
Ward Green Primary School

THE STARS IN THE SKY

Turn off your lights,
Go outside,
Get the telescope,
Look up,
You will see,
Lots and lots of shining stars,
Wow,
Stare closely
You could see anything
Maybe a shooting star
Or maybe you will see a bottle,
Or even a car,
Most of the days,
I go outside and look up at the stars,
Every night I see something different,
I think of my family who are up there,
I know that they are looking down on me,
And I love them.

Connor Johnson (9)
Ward Green Primary School

A BIRD'S LIFE

I fly free up in the sky
My wings outstretched
My beak up high
I look for food
I sing my song,
I fly around all day long,
I do not worry
No cares I have except for the cat but he cannot fly,
Up in the tree I make my nest
And when darkness falls it's time to rest.
When the dawn breaks I will awake
I'll sing my song and fly around
And watch all the people on the ground.
A nice person may put out some scraps
But I will have to beat that cat
Is he watching me I do not know
But I know he can be slow.
I'll swoop down and get the scraps
Oops be careful he might snap
But he cannot fly that stupid cat
Back to my nest I must go
I'll rest my wings
And eat my scraps
And sing a song to that stupid cat.
A busy day I have had
But I am a bird and I am glad.

Jack Hague (10)
Ward Green Primary School

WEATHER

Where does the wind come from?
The wind comes from a rough storm at sea that none can control;
Tossed high into the valleys and peaks.

How hot does the sun shine?
The sun shines as hot as a dragon's burning breath
That coats every corner of the Earth.

How do we get thunder?
We get thunder when a great rolling stampede
Travels across the Earth's plains.

What are hailstones?
Hailstones are the frozen tears of the sobbing Ice God.

What is the sun?
The sun is a great burning ball of fire
Smiling back to us on Earth.

Holly Kilburn (11)
Ward Green Primary School

KITTENS WAYS

Kittens are small,
Kittens are cute,
Kittens like playing with balls of wool
They chase it around and tangle things up
They better watch out that you don't trip up.

Dominic Holmes (9)
Ward Green Primary School

DOGS

Dogs are animals that growl and bark
But are lots of fun when you take them in the park.

Watch them run after a ball
They never listen to you when you call.

See them play, running and jumping,
When they stop their hearts are thumping.

They get excited and run and run,
Playing with dogs is such good fun.

Yes, dogs are great
Dogs are super,
But don't forget the pooper scooper!

Siobhan Crabtree (9)
Ward Green Primary School

FLOWERS

Flowers can be yellow,
Flowers can be red,
Flowers can be alive,
Flowers can be dead.

Flowers are usually bright,
Flowers can be beautiful,
Flowers like the light,
Flowers can be dull.

Daniel Connolly (10)
Ward Green Primary School

WINTER

Snow as high as the treetops
Freezing into ice,
Its beauty like a star,
Winter . . . winter . . .

The robin puffs up his bright red breast,
Guarding the precious nuts and seeds,
It's like a red for danger warning,
Winter . . . winter . . .

The hurtling winds,
Thrashing rain and sleet,
It's like pins and needles on my face,
Winter . . . winter . . .

The sun stays low in the sky,
With blinding light that stops me seeing,
It's like the Devil's cave,
Winter . . . winter . . .

Waves crashing on rocks,
Seas climbing the high cliffs,
It's like a raging monster,
Winter . . . winter . . .

Flowering bulbs beneath the solid ground,
Push up their flowering stems,
It's like there's something changing,
Winter . . . winter . . .

I think you're on your way out!

Grace Jenkinson (10)
Ward Green Primary School

CANDLES

A candle flickers in the dark
Glows orange, red and makes a spark
The flames appear to be dancing and twirling
You can see the fire in your eyes burning
It looks so spooky in the night
A candle looks like a bright star in moonlight
Some candles give off lovely scents
But when they melt they can go bent.
If you blow it it goes out
You're in the dark scream and shout
The wax is melting drip, drip, drip
The flame goes out bit by bit!

Laura Hutchinson (10)
Ward Green Primary School

WEATHER POETRY

Where does the wind come from?
The wind comes from a locked away cupboard
Far away beyond Earth, blown from the mouths of God
Covering the world with its icy touch.

Why does the wind blow hard?
The wind blows hard to rid the Earth of human misfortune
Separating the toils of a sunless world.

What is rain?
Rain is the angry tears of the locked away Sun God,
Crying to be released from the deep, dark dungeon.

What is the sun?
The sun is the God's fire pushing the heat down
Onto the dark, dull Earth
Making it reveal light.

What is lightning?
Lightning is a witch casting a spell over the world.

Kimberley Mills (11)
Ward Green Primary School

GYMNAST

Bar swinger,
Hand clinger,
Floor tumbler,
Quiet mumbler,
Vault jumper,
Floor bumper,
Beam faller,
Cartwheel crawler,
Graceful glider,
Mistake hider,
Olympic winner,
Big grinner,
Audience loud,
Family proud.

Jessica Myatt (11)
Ward Green Primary School

LISTEN

Listen to the wind
As it blows with a grin
It is sharp as a pin
Listen to the wind.

Listen to the rain
As it trickles down the pane
As fast as a train
Listen to the rain.

Listen to the wind
As it blows with a grin
It is sharp as a pin
Listen, listen, listen to the wind.

Megan Cunningham (8)
Ward Green Primary School

MY GUITAR

My guitar plays a tune,
Also the strings look like a baboon.
My guitar shines so bright,
Always in the starry night.
My guitar pulls my hair,
And when it does it I look like a bear.
My guitar likes to sing,
Even when I pluck its strings.
My guitar likes to play
And then it sleeps in the hay.
My guitar goes to school,
And it plays in the swimming pool.
My guitar eats some sweets,
And when it does it, it weeps.
And my guitar has a daughter
Even when it shouldn't oughter.

Laura Barnes-Martin (8)
Ward Green Primary School

WAR POEM

Dead bodies lying on the ground
Blood squirting all around,
Shotguns firing bullets in the air.
Children and mothers watching in despair,
Husbands dying
While wives are crying.
Lots of people getting injured
They get their medicine through syringes.
Nurses giving out plasters
War is a horrible disaster!

Bradley Mellor & Joe Halstead (11)
Ward Green Primary School

THE BEAST

It was big and scary and very, very hairy.
The beast, the beast it would make you into a feast.
It was big and round and stood fifteen feet off the ground.

It would stand looking at you
Like some sort of confused animal trapped in a zoo.
It would scream and shout
Trying to get out.
Just so it could capture you!

If it got out *you* would scream and shout
So that it would not capture you.
The beast, the beast
Let it stop in the zoo!

Daniel Riches (8)
Ward Green Primary School

PARTY TIME

Food and games and lots of fun,
The party now has just begun.
Bangers bang and poppers pop,
Now it's started the fun won't stop.

Musical Chairs, Tail On The Donkey,
With all that food the table must be wonkey.
Rap and funk, dance and hip-hop,
Now it's ended you just might flop.

Daniel Brown (9)
Ward Green Primary School

TREASURE

Treasure, treasure under the sea
What have you got just for me?
Golden jewels,
Red or blue,
Silver diamonds
For me and you.

Kelly Hayes (8)
Ward Green Primary School

FOOTBALL

When I walk through the tunnel to see the roaring crowd
I like scoring the golden goal as I sing I shout,
When I am sent off my world will come to an end until
I run on the field to sing and shout again . . .
My favourite team is Leeds United as they thrash the world.

Joel Bragg (11)
West Road Primary School

IMAGINE

Imagine a snail
As big as a whale.
Imagine a lark
As big as a shark.
Imagine a mouse,
As big as a house.
Imagine a snake
As small as a snowflake.
Imagine a frog
As long as a log.
Imagine a bee
As big as a tree
And a flea as big as me.

Luke Hawson (11)
West Road Primary School

FOOTBALL

English players eating healthy,
All their teams are very wealthy.

I like people scoring goals,
Not when the ball gets stuck in holes.

I like watching games,
I remember all their names.

I like seeing the cup
Especially when they hold it up.

My best team is Liverpool
They are very, very cool.

Scott Rhodes (11)
West Road Primary School

RESIDENT EVIL 2

Evil is dark as Hell,
It smells like blood.
Evil sounds like children screaming,
It feels like sharp knives.
Evil lives in souls.

Zachary Samuels-Price (10)
West Road Primary School

LOVE POEM

Love is good to me
It's in my heart every day.

Love means a lot to me
It's with me every day.

Byron Crowther (11)
West Road Primary School

WINNIE THE POOH

Winnie The Pooh
Tigger and crew,
Had a laugh,
Went to the zoo.

When they came back,
They had a bath,
And that is Winnie The Pooh,
Tigger and crew.

Wendy Holmes & Kirsty Tomlinson (11)
West Road Primary School

BEST MATES

Best mates don't fight,
They play along all day.
They have parties all night,
Have a laugh on their way.

Best mates don't fight,
They have a game of tug of war.
They tell ghost stories in a dim light
As they tell them Mum says,
'Shut that door.'

Best friends never fight.

Robyn Astill & Terri Garth (11)
West Road Primary School

WINTER

A cool breeze is blowing,
Trees are waving cautiously.
Snowflakes falling softly,
Stranger tramping through the snow.
Ground hard and frozen now,
Colours faded from view.
Flowers are here no more,
Snow falls down in torrents.
Icicles appear from nowhere,
Grey clouds rule over the sky now.
A winter's night is cold and dull,
Spring will surely come.

Laura Brandon (11)
West Road Primary School